THE WHOLE ISLAND

Simon Maddrell is a queer Manx poet, performer, editor and facilitator living in Brighton and Hove.

He is published in sixteen anthologies and numerous literary journals, including *Poetry Wales*, *The Rialto*, *Ambit*, *Butcher's Dog*, *Ink Sweat and Tears*, *Long Poem Magazine*, *Stand*, *The Moth* and *Under the Radar*.

Simon's debut pamphlet, *Throatbone*, was published in 2020 by UnCollected Press. His second, *Queerfella*, jointly-won The Rialto Open Pamphlet Competition 2020.

With the poets Vasiliki Albedo and Mary Mulholland, Simon's work appeared in the anthologies *All About Our Mothers* (2022) and *All About Our Fathers* (2023), published by Nine Pens Press.

Simon's Manx queer history pamphlet, *Isle of Sin*, was published by Polari Press in March 2023.

The Whole Island
Yn Slane Ellan

Simon Maddrell

Supported by

Valley Press

First published in 2023 by Valley Press
Woodend, The Crescent, Scarborough, YO11 2PW
www.valleypressuk.com

ISBN 978-1-915606-29-7
Cat. no. VP0220

Copyright © Simon Maddrell 2023

The right of Simon Maddrell to be identified as the
author of this work has been asserted in accordance with
the Copyright, Designs and Patents Act 1988.

All rights reserved. No part of this publication may be
reproduced, stored in or introduced into a retrieval system,
or transmitted in any form, by any means (electronic,
mechanical, photocopying, recording or otherwise) without
prior written permission from the rights holders.

A CIP record for this book is available from the British Library.

Culture Vannin has provided funding only and the views,
opinions, findings and conclusions or recommendations
expressed are strictly those of the author. Culture Vannin
takes no responsibility for any errors or omissions or for the
correctness of the information contained in this publication.

Cover image: modified Copernicus Sentinel data 2018 (ESA).
Cover and text design by Jamie McGarry.
Editorial consultant: Kate Simpson.

Printed and bound in Great Britain by
Imprint Digital, Upton Pyne, Exeter.

going home

is the same whichever
way we go by air or by sea
we risk the same as we do
in love either to crash &
burn or drown instead
to lose our self and hence
to lose our love perhaps
both asked & answered.
here is the rub

for whatever we lose
(like a you or a me)
it's always ourselves
we find in the sea.

— e e cummings

Contents

Foddeeaght 9

Manannan mac y Leir 10

Puffin Mother 11

Crosh Cuirn 12

In nineteen ninety-one I stepped out of my skin 13

According to the signs 14

For the Future Manx Explorer 15

Treisht 16

Shipwrighting 17

The Vikings didn't need roads 18

Yn Slane Ellan 19

A Locksmith's Tower 22

Oology 23

Our language drips 24

Calls from the Edge 25

Cronk Meayll 26

Twelve Graves 27

Beauty makes our little island an everywhere 28

One thing leads to another 29

And when I look back 30

Notes on the poems 31

Acknowledgements 36

Foddeeaght

He asks if I yearn for it,
if we have a word for it, like Hiraeth,

how he feels when away from his other
Celtic home, and I brush it off

like a speck of fluff, as if it's obvious
a queer would hate being kept

in a beautifully busy cottage, tucked away
in a private bay below Milner's Tower —

it's a folly, to think I want to be
where he is, to think I could

add anything to this, like my pride
in having scuba-dived the world over,

in the marine biology station here at Port Erin.
How it's now closed.

Foddeeaght Hiraeth Homesickness, nostalgia and longing

Manannan mac y Leir

Nothing has changed. Mourning
a ruined family, his lost humanity
inflicting wounds on the Otherworld.

His tears, pearls that fled the sea
turn into that single mountain island
where I was raised from my mother's

womb, gasping for life in a tent
for seven days, seven years or seven
score months, I now forget. When

I cried it was on the inside, growing
a cardiac rock with lichen cracks
and moss where I weep.

Manannan mac y Leir Son of the Sea, Lord of Mann

Puffin Mother

You abandoned the nest, left our sanctuary, pushed away by the ironfella also eating up puffinus puffinus who only appears to be you.

We perched plastic models to bring you back — better versions of ourselves — perfect in the way no offspring can be. We played sounds

of domestic bliss borrowed from a faraway colony. We lined up loudspeakers atop the cliffs like a picket fence singing apple pie.

Whether due to this highly fabricated world or roddan's absence you returned, not home exactly, because you were a different mother.

But you came back just the same, and are in fact still here, even so long since you went away.

Ironfella, Roddan Rattus norvegicus / *Puffinus puffinus* Manx shearwater

Crosh Cuirn

The remnants of sheep's wool untwisted from brambles + barbed wire twisted around two broken twigs of rowan cuirn, the mountain ash, to make a cross that wards off those drogh spyrrydyn, a crosh without nails for May Day Eve.

The remnants of Manx folklore unravelled from forgotten stories + memories tangled around two broken wings of the ferrish themselves — a childhood stolen to make a cross to ward off all his filthy thinking, a crosh with nails piercing his bubbling spirit

left hanging with primroses on both doors. He dances around that rowan in the garden, his purple gansee snagging with every turn, he scoffs jam bonnag whilst red berries last. A green jacket swishes on a dragonfly's back as a dooinney beg doffs their rose petal cap.

Crosh Cuirn Rowan Cross
drogh spyrrydyn evil spirits / *gansee* sweater / *bonnag* Manx cake
ferrish, themselves fairies / *dooinney beg* little fella

In nineteen ninety-one I stepped out of my skin

for the first time
there was a young man
sucking a cock
like he'd arrived back home at last

not in the sense of the seventies
oblong blocks
of Manx Ices, unwrapped
and shoved into a round cone

but more so that rocket lolly,
you remember,
wide at the bottom, ridged
with a sweet-lipped tip

of white chocolate.
The nineties wonder
at what dialling 0898 offered
— cool, fresh & wild for it

until just after that
moment of melting white,
hundreds & thousands flashed by
— now too exposed

to survive so raw,
I crawled back into my skin, sagging
& dragging itself to the bathroom
— then I threw up.

According to the signs

The footpath to Port Willin is not passable at high water.
My mind floods & races with anticipation

as I circle the sea-walled Raad ny Foillan passing under
a civil war battery like we face in our own islands,

the unoccupied land where I find a tiny bathing creek
— looking purpose-made for the likes of us —

private and delicious like the young men I imagine
in this cove, a secret space to be ourselves with care-

less abandon and timely attention to all the tides
flowing inside, even rippling in our deepness,

one could be left alone with the only escape being
those uphill trails to Gob ny Rona — paths within

bracken and olden woods — a maze hiding
many answers and trees with many arms.

Raad ny Foillan The Way of the Gull / *Gob ny Rona* Point of the Seals

For the Future Manx Explorer

Hail the explorer born amidst gorse
and heather, fearing we miss the other
then three kisses blow across your brow
these murmured spells of mine

find silence in a cacophony of inward
voices amongst outward noises.
Like *The Faerie Queene*, I can help you
dress the awful beauty of naked bones,

to unleash that red-billed chough, sing
trench deep within the soil that bore you,
toil, toil, deeper than death, dig till spade
clangs. Our dialects soaked in spes altera.

Polari is choked, Old Manx wanes,
both dying in a tholtan — lift the latch.

after T. E. Brown

spes altera hope for another / *tholtan* ruined cottage

Treisht

A three-legged man was bored
of the island and caught a ship
through the universe where he
reached a dark puddle
standing on one leg, another lagging,
shaking between fear and anticipation,
the third leg stepped into the puddle,

this leg certain it wasn't a black hole,
after all there was no event horizon,
meaning the puddle edges didn't glow.
However, his mother popped up
and said, *only the boring get bored.*

So, the man, with all those legs intact,
came back to the island and visited
all of the places he ever loved
on the edge of everywhere
there is always something new
and all the scenes we've played before
never feel the same.

Treisht Trust, hope & confidence

Shipwrighting

I wish I could build a ship — so when *Mona's Isle*
iron-paddle steams after 1860 no-one will rename her
Ellan Vannin, and she will no longer lose thirty-six lives,

sixty sheep, ninety bags of moots and a grand piano
in a screw-driven sorrowful crossing — their offspring
will be known as 'The Manx Generation'. The second

ship I wish to build will not be renamed *Golden Hind,*
nor will it claim to discover anywhere, neither will our
own vanquish be celebrated by building *Odin's Raven.*

You will see no ship called *Kitty's Amelia* sail back in
1807 to 'abstract' enslaved people from Bonny Island,
as eighty Manx captains like Hugh Crow already had.

Instead, the next ship I build will be *Mona's Queen.*
I'll make her with wood to escape a 1940 magnetic mine
— saving twenty-four crew from a war-sunk sea-grave.

After saving 25,000 men from Dunkirk, all those Manx
ships and boats will save ten thousand more, then more
than *Mona's* starboard anchor will rest at Kallow Point.

I do not know the name for these acts of sacrifice and
service to a conquering ruler, but I wish I could build
a word for it and give it an iron mast and anchors —

like that ghostly hulk where those onboard only see
Death and Life-in-Death thrive. We may grieve, but
not as those who have no hope on a nameless ship.

moots turnips

The Vikings didn't need roads

to plunder and burn
wooden vessels
graves not tricks
a queer-shaped ball kicked
about and back and over that wall
without the love of Antinoös
rich dukes envied
its land and its rights
no sooner grasped than sold
to be owned by George III in 1765
a hanging chalice
freedom is an oxymoron
flourishing is a drag queen
owning herself.

Yn Slane Ellan

after Virgilio Piñera

The charm of water hangs around my neck. If I thought the waters encircling me weren't maternal fluid, I'd never sleep. If I thought this island was a cancer that ate my father's bones, I'd never return home. I've stood where my father was born and where he's buried, I still see his sun-burnt wrinkles skeeting the horizon.

I have fished off breakwater & boat for mackerel, a lesser substitute for herring, but stronger in the tug when hooked. He pickled pots of them for hours, his breaded cud preceded the self-judged announcement of its relative success.

I watched him unscrew a brass doorknob at the ruining farmhouse in Grenaby, a sense of entitlement common to this island. What is fifty years of belonging to someone else when it was ours for two hundred more? Whose island is this anyway? A colonial haven came & went, came & lent & sold with scattered remnants. Our island is almost too old to define itself.

Heeyn y slane ellan roin. The daily mist, the nightly fog, the wet is always fifteen minutes from the sun and twelve minutes from the wind. All the land's weather is underfoot, but on the sea it floats & swirls & sinks. Complacency is our greatest risk.

yn slane ellan the whole island
skeeting looking
heeyn y slane ellan roin the whole of the island lay before us

My brother was stung by a scorpion in a Ghanaian sandpit before he sat on a beach. A woman who no longer shares my name came back & went, whilst the other two of us never lived back, although one lies here dead. All of this is to say, that some drown in the sea and some drown on land, whilst others just love to swim.

I remember the old woman who was surrounded by water for a hundred years and was questioned about her belief in "fairies." She scowled at the TV presenter, "Of course not!" she snapped, but in our next breath she assured us "they are there just the same."

I linger over Manx food — queen scallops, licked rock & kippers. From the rowing boat, I pick mussels one by one from the iron pier in search of music like sea, sugar & smoke. We boil them in sea water & white wine, I imagine this is what being a grown-up is like, and I still wish that it's true.

Here, the island's people sacrifice their livers and hunt for liverworts in glens. There was once a clear Manx whiskey that lost its name in court for not being brown and now it's called Manx Blue. To say its people are alcoholics clinging to a rock is drogh-ellynagh.

mooinjer veggey little people, fairies
drogh-ellynagh rude

I find freedom in my cocoon, if only for a while. I go south digging potatoes, flint arrows, and horse bones hoping for something else. When I reach Cregneish, Uncle Stan rips up that letter from British royalty to light a fire and then shares the story about the gold-laden Spanish galleon and The Drinking Dragon off Yn Cholloo. The lookout crew were so scared by its fiery breath, it was too late for the captain & too late for the rocks. There is a freedom in imagining the truth and remembering it too.

Eternal histories of Vikings & Druids who were, and Celts who weren't, or the other way around, or any way at all — *Quocunque Jeceris Stabit*. There is a reason why the Romans never made it across to Manannan's isle. There is also a reason we captained the ships but no reason for "the necessary evil" of Captain Crow. Eternal histories we cannot judge, or change, until we remember.

In the time it took illegal boys to be legal men, twelve died for being bent. The chug of the drowned gay boy's car still hums on the seafront. The hosepipe washed up like driftwood on the beach, his shoes on the Tower of Refuge rocks. These eternal histories of shame. If only those boys walked freely, like after those internment camp fences were taken down.

South of Eary Cushlin, the hen harrier soars above the hollow where the chapel lies, evading persecution like the monks of old, feeding on meadow pipits & voles. On the edge of extinction, on the edge of the whole island, the edge of our language hovers.

Yn Cholloo Calf of Man
Quocunque Jeceris Stabit Whithersoever way you throw it, it will stand
Manannan Son of the Sea, Lord of Mann

A Locksmith's Tower

Our walk began in Bradda Glen,
dappled leaves patchwork
my bare skin, mulch tramples
turn to a moorland trek,
little, when little, did I know that
this imposing tower overlooking
my idyllic bay was not a castle but
built to honour a locksmith's gifts.
Four kids chasing ahead
parents ambling along
when all of a sudden
in our desire to hide,
I dived spread-eagled
onto gorse not thinking,
or assuming it was heather,
I forget which, like
sometimes we don't
know what we are doing
when we haul herring
instead of mackerel.
The consequences
for the boy
with exposed
flesh was indelible
red spots, wet eyes
& other laughs.
Funny how such dies
are cast, how
history repeats like
a kippered
burp.

Oology

My father collected bird eggs as a kid
so avidly I think he was an oologist.

His sister discovered she really liked seagull eggs
— boiled not sunny, runny, not hatched —

I had a few, quite a few

He snatched them for her from cliffs above Port Erin
a hobby that he passed down to his middle son —
I was awe-struck at his collection's rarities

he had a few, quite a few

which reminds me of all the wine I've drunk
so avidly I thought I was an enologist.

I had a few, quite a few

My sister suggested I quit. Celts are prone to iron
retention in blood, the only solution being its
letting, the way family ties can be diluted.

Ta fuill ny s'chee na ushtey

not wanting to die thirsty

but with red lips.

Ta fuill ny s'chee na ushtey Blood is thicker than water

Our language drips

in the dark   I am afraid   of meeting
my emptiness   but I must
return   to the isle of my birth
before I become   my own extinction.
Our native Yn Gaelg
was nearly silenced
from what   only it   can express.

I nearly zipped   my own lips
in a black-bagged lack   of understanding
that it is language   that restores our place
that speaks louder   than any plinth
that   when it cries   deepens the sea.

It is near impossible   to describe the sun
rising   but it is possible   to feel
the language   of the sun
setting   on darkness.

Yn Gaelg Manx Gaelic

Calls from the Edge

We-ow-we — We-ow-we — We-ow-we — We-ow-we

Sumatran cuckoo	calls from the edge	two-footed
grounded	as the Manx shearwater	black & white
dodo threat	reflects humanity's island	inside
· lilac-eyes	draining to purpled blood &	rattus rattus
poison-mixed peril	looking beyond her	crown
plucking & picking	spineless creatures	wrapped
beneath waved	leaves a lesser-seen	cuckoo
island-gifted nest the	universe	its home
menaced tigers	& drowning dragons	trapped
virid-coated cameras	within	hidden
russet-chested	wounding stabs	in green
existence	no-one listens to	calls from the edge

Oo-weh — Oo-weh — Cuc-cuk-coo — Rahrrr — Rahrrr

Cronk Meayll

      rock crystal centre of the bald hill
      graves wherever I stare to balance
     feet teeter & scratch on the edge
    eyes close to a howling sun & nose
  sea-smelt breeze of gorse flowers
heather with undertones of sheep

in a red darkness, like whirlwinds
   species after species extinguish
      in meteor showers of visions
         ancestors float above twelve
            graves, hands shaking, heads
               shivering at all we've yet to do

Cronk Meayll Mull Hill, literally bald hill

Twelve Graves

        circle of   crown

       connected   spirit

third eye   beyond

  sees   the

     dark   charred bone

        matter   of death

Beauty makes our little island an everywhere

our little time an everywhen,
our struggles are both won & lost
when poison flows too freely,
sheep roam the hills, glens
riddle with venal streams.

And there we sit staring into space,
two fools I know to be a little wise
in a lovewreck full of air & fairies
dancing in shapeless harmony.

No poppies or charms will bring
sleep nor crystals keep us awake.
No elixir so silken it will soothe
every river's throat, nor alchemy

so strong to turn iron into bullets
for life's own fate whose end
will do us little proud
for it diminishes everything

and everywhen, our affair is to be
greater, a million armies returning
life to what it was centuries before
& centuries after that tree
whose fig unveiled ego & greed.

after John Donne

One thing leads to another

— as in sex.
Manx shearwaters
maraud land & sea
like Vikings & rodents

— eat & be eaten.
Ship-shed predators
with burrowed lunches
of puffins, eaten too

        like krill   pieces of plastic
        floating clear & yellow & pink

— as in pink penguin shit.
Chick stomachs loaded
with glitter   although not
in bioluminescent stress

        like krill   digest plastic pieces
        floating past & present & future

— eat & be eaten.
Stuck in the gut & gullet
others nourish the seabed
with carbon & foreplay

        — as in sex. Eggs rise
        to the surface   like plastic
        pieces   the new fossils
        floating past our survival.

And when I look back

across that sea
waves are still falling
sometimes pushed
others pulled
bobbing in the slack.

And all these moments
bubbles & froth
becomes wind
just blowing
over & short enough.

And looking forward
is the same, but only just
for the time of our being.

'And when you look back it's all like a puff,
Happy and over and short enough.'
Betsy Lee, T. E. Brown

Notes on the poems

Translations are from Yn Gaelg [Manx Gaelic] unless otherwise stated.

FODDEEAGHT

Foddeeaght: *Hiraeth* [Welsh]: Homesickness, nostalgia, longing.

MANANNAN MAC Y LEIR

Manannan mac y Leir: Manannán mac Lir [Celtic]: Little Manann, Son of the Sea, warrior and King of the Otherworld.

PUFFIN MOTHER

Puffinus puffinus [Latin]: Manx shearwater

Roddan: Ironfella [Manx dialect]: *Rattus rattus* [Latin] — it is bad luck in the Isle of Man to use its common English name.

Rattus norvegicus is the specific species on the Calf of Man responsible for eating Manx Shearwaters and Puffin chicks, causing them to leave the region. Following a programme to eradicate *rattus* species, an annual "decoy puffin" project was set up in 2016, which places models on clifftops along with a sound system playing the bird's call in a bid to attract them back to nest. On the Calf of Man, the puffins declined from a population high of 60 pairs in 1979 until the last breeding pair was recorded in the late 1980s — they have now returned for the first time in 34 years, and shearwater numbers have grown too.

CROSH CUIRN

A unique Manx tradition on *Oie Voaldyn* [May Day Eve] is to make a *Crosh Cuirn* [a Rowan Cross] from Mountain Ash twigs to ward off evil spirits or for good luck, often hung with primrose flowers on front and back doors.

drogh spyrrydyn: evil spirits; *gansee:* sweater; *bonnag:* Manx cake, bun.

Ferrish [fairies] also known in Manx dialect as *themselves* or in Manx Gaelic as *mooinjer veggey* [little people] or *dooinney beg* [little fella].

In nineteen ninety-one I stepped out of my skin

Manx Ices was an Isle of Man ice cream company using full cream and eggs, which was unusual in the British Isles in the 1970s and 80s.

0898: a premium cost telephone line often used as a (sex) dating service.

According to the signs

Port Willin is better known as Port e Vullen — according to the signs.

Raad ny Foillan: literally 'The Way of the Gull' the name for the Isle of Man coastal path.

Gob ny Rona: Point of the Seals or 'headland of the division' between Port e Vullen and Port Lewaigue.

For the Future Manx Explorer

This poem is inspired by, and borrows lines & words from 'Spes Altera, To The Future Manx Poet' T. E. Brown (1830-1897).

The Faerie Queene is an English epic poem by Edmund Spenser first published in 1590, then republished in 1596 in longer form.

Spes altera [Latin]: Hope for another.

Polari is a form of slang or cant used in British circus, wrestler, sailor, criminals, sex worker and gay subcultures.

Tholtan: ruined cottage

Treisht

Treisht: trust, hope & confidence

Shipwrighting

'Yet sorrow not as those who have no hope' is from the poem 'Sorrowful crossing' by Cushag (Josephine Kermode, 1852-1937) about the shipwreck of *Ellan Vannin* (formerly named *Mona's Isle*) in Liverpool Bay, Dec. 3rd 1909.

Golden Hind was a galleon captained by Francis Drake in his circumnavigation of the world between 1577 and 1580. She was originally known as *Pelican*, but Drake renamed her mid-voyage in 1578, in honour of his patron, Sir Christopher Hatton, whose crest was a golden hind (a female red deer).

Odin's Raven is a two-thirds scale replica of the *Gokstad ship*, which was sailed from Trondheim to Peel, Isle of Man, by a joint Manx and Norwegian crew. The project formed part of the 1979 Manx Millennium Celebrations,

Kitty's Amelia is the slave ship captained by the Manxman Hugh Crow whose memoir was published in 1830.

'Death and Life-in-Death' and the (nameless) 'ghostly hulk' are from the *Rime of the Ancient Mariner* (Samuel Coleridge, 1798).

THE VIKINGS DIDN'T NEED ROADS

In the *Collection of Old Manx Songs and Ballads*, T. E. Brown wrote about the relatively small number of Manx songs, "The football position of the island, kicked about from Celt to Norseman, from English to Scot. This must have affected the language as well as the temper and spirit of the people."

Antinoös [Ancient Greek]: *Antinoüs* [Latin]: Antonius was the lover of Emperor Hadrian, who built the eponymous wall separating England and Scotland.

George III was King of Great Britain and Ireland (1760-1820).

The Isle of Man Purchase Act 1765, also known as the Act of Revestment, purchased the feudal rights of the Dukes of Atholl as Lords of Man over the Isle of Man, and revested them into the British Crown for a sum of £70,000. The Act did not go as far as had been proposed: for a period there had been plans to merge the Isle of Man into the English county of Cumberland.

The Isle of Man Government launched a new brand identity in 2006: *Giving you Freedom to Flourish*.

YN CLANE ELLAN THE WHOLE ISLAND

After 'La Isla en Peso' by Virgilio Piñera, 1968. Translated as *The Whole Island* by Mark Weiss, Shearsman, 2010.

skeeting [Manx dialect]: looking.

Heeyn y slane ellan roin: The whole of the island lay before us.

Mooinjer veggey: literally little people, British common name is fairies.

'The Drinking Dragon' is an islet off the Calf of Man, which gets its name from how it looks from a certain angle.

Yn Cholloo: Calf of Man — the largest of three small islands in waters surrounding Mannin.

Quocunque Jeceris Stabit [Latin]: 'Whithersoever way you throw it, it will stand' — the motto of the Isle of Man.

Manannan mac y Leir: Son of the Sea, King of the Otherworld.

The Manx Captain Hugh Crow viewed "the abstraction of slaves from Africa to our (sic) colonies as a necessary evil."

Below Eary Cushlin is the site of a chapel and hermit's cottage called *Lag ny Keeilly*, which means Hollow of the Chapel.

A Locksmith's Tower

after Milner's Tower, Bradda Head, Port Erin. Milner's Tower was erected in 1871, designed the shape of a key to honour the local philanthropist and benefactor, William Milner (1804-1874), who was a wealthy safe-maker who moved from Liverpool in the mid-1800s. with particular care for the local fishermen and impoverished families. By 1871, Milner was so beloved among the community that a tower was commissioned and funded by private donations to honour his contributions to the people of Port Erin.

Our language drips

Yn Gaelg is Manx Gaelic.

Manx is a Gaelic language closely related to both Irish and Scottish Gaelic. It was first brought to the shores of the island by Irish monks and merchants in the fourth and fifth centuries AD, as Christianity spread northwards. Manx began to emerge as a distinct language when the last King of Mann died in 1265 and the island came under the control of Scotland. Manx was pronounced a "dead language" in 1974 after the last native speaker, Ned Maddrell, passed away. In succession to this in 2009, Manx Language was officially defined as "extinct" by UNESCO but now has a new categorization as a "revitalized" language. Around 2,200 people are now able to speak, read or write in Manx, according to the 2021 Census.

CALLS FROM THE EDGE

The author's phonetic interpretation of the following bird call sounds:

Sumatran Ground Cuckoo: *We-ow-we—We-ow-we —We-ow-we —We-ow-we*

Manx Shearwater: *Oo-weh — Oo-weh — Cuc-cuk-coo — Rahrrr — Rahrrr*

CRONK MEAYLL, TWELVE GRAVES

Cronk Meayll: Mull Hill (literally bald hill) is the site of Meayll Circle near to Cregneish, Isle of Man — a late Neolithic or early Bronze Age circle (c. 3,500 BC) consisting of six pairs of cists or graves called *Rhullick-y-lagg-shliggagh* [graveyard of the valley of broken slates].

BEAUTY MAKES OUR LITTLE ISLAND AN EVERYWHERE

After John Donne (1572-1631). Borrows words & phrases from the following: Air and Angels; Holy Sonnets; Metempsychosis; No Man is an Island; The First Anniversary; The Good-Morrow; To Sir Edward Hubert at Juliers.

ONE THING LEADS TO ANOTHER

Plastic ingestion was investigated in an internationally-important breeding population of Manx Shearwaters on Skomer Island, Wales in 2018–19. Plastic was found in 71% of stomach contents (68% adults, 75% fledglings). Seabirds may ingest plastic either directly, often mistaking plastic for potential prey items, or indirectly via filter-feeding organisms and other prey species such as krill.

'Plastic ingestion in adult and fledgling Manx Shearwaters *Puffinus puffinus* on Skomer Island, Wales', *Seabird, The Journal of Seabird Group*, Issue 34, 2022.

Acknowledgements

Thanks to the editors of the following for publishing the poems below or previous versions of them.

Under the Radar, Nine Arches Press, Spring 2023 — 'In nineteen ninety-one I stepped out of my skin'

Amethyst Review, 11th March 2023 — 'Calls from the Edge'

Amethyst Review, 3rd February 2023 — 'Cronk Meayll'

berlin lit, Issue 2, December 2022 — 'Foddeeaght'

The Four Faced Liar, Issue 1, November 2022 — 'Our language drips'

Long Poem Magazine, Issue 26, Autumn 2021 — 'The Whole Island'

The Dawntreader, Indigo Dreams, Issue 55, July 2021 — 'Twelve Graves'

Brittle Star Magazine, Issue 46, June 2020 — 'Crosh Cuirn'

'For the Future Manx Explorer' is a different version of 'For the Future Manx Poet' from the chapbook *Throatbone,* Uncollected Press, July 2020.

Thank You

With grateful thanks to publisher Jamie McGarry, my editor Kate Simpson and Culture Vannin without whom, whichsoever way one looks at it, this book would not exist. And, for all those who helped one way or another: Brighton Poetry Stanza, Covent Garden Poetry Stanza, The Crocodile Collective, Rob Hamberger, Mari Hughes-Edwards, Ruth Keggin Gell, Ann Kinvig, Annie Kissack, Martin Lyons, Breesha Maddrell, John Maddrell, Manx Museum, Manx LitFest, New Writing South, Barbara Qualtrough, Jeanette & Will Qualtrough, Royal Literary Fund, Alan Shea, Chris Sheard, SKEGS, Society of Authors, Ahren Warner et al.